CYBERSAFE

what you need to know to safely navigate the Internet

Quillquest Books

USA

Quillquest Books

A division of the Quillquest Publishing Co.

Quillquest Books, Quillquest Junior Books, Quillquest Classic Books, and the sailing quill are the exclusive trademarks of the Quillquest Publishing Co., Quillquest Enterprises, Virginia, USA. For information or comment regarding this book contact: Quillquestbooks@msn.com

ISBN 978-0-940075-08-5

CYBERSAFE

what you need to know to safely
navigate the Internet

edited by

frank mosco

Contents

The Connection; How to Go Online - 10

Cyberspeak; Learning the Language - 16

Site Seeing On The Internet - 22

Privacy on the Internet - 32

Security on the Internet - 35

Online Security & Safety Tips - 40

Beware the Dotcons - 50

Fraud: Avoiding Internet Investment Scams - 57

Using the Internet to Invest Wisely - 60

You've Got Spam; How to "Can" Unwanted E-mail - 75

Resources - 82

Welcome to Cyberspace

Cyberspace *is a domain characterized by the use of electronics and the electromagnetic spectrum to store, modify, and exchange data via networked systems and associated physical infrastructures.*

Wikapedia the Free (cyberspace) Encyclopedia

Wow, what a mouthful and if we all had to think of the Internet in those terms how many of us would actually run in the other direction? The word "cyberspace" (from *cybernetics* and *space*) was coined by science fiction novelist and seminal cyberpunk author William Gibson in his 1982 story "Burning Chrome" and popularized by his 1984 novel *Neuromancer*. The portion of *Neuromancer* cited in this respect is usually the following:

> *Cyberspace. A consensual hallucination experienced daily by billions of legitimate operators, in every nation, by children being taught mathematical concepts... A graphic representation of data abstracted from banks of every computer in the human system. Unthinkable complexity. Lines of light ranged in the nonspace of the mind, clusters and constellations of data. Like city lights, receding...*

Even artistically spoken of in a novel the concept of the World Wide Web, the *Internet*, can be intimidating and confusing to say the least. And though it has existed long enough now to initiate changes in our personal and professional lives, not to mention national and world affairs, there are many of you who have only just come to use and hopefully embrace it. To you the Internet is new and exciting, and yes, regardless of your age be it 6 or 60, it can also be exceedingly challenging.

People love to apply rules to every new concept or technology that comes down the road and the Internet, which now influences so much of our world, is no exception. A principal difference regarding the internet however is that it is indeed a world wide confluence that knows no borders and no boundaries, meaning it can be a wonderful experience or dangerous and disappointing one depending on your knowledge and ability to use it. What this also means is that though there are technical rules and standards that govern the operation of the Internet there are also few rules that govern the content and the actions of users of the Internet. In a way it is like sailing in dangerous international waters where no one governs or rules over anything more than their own ship. Knowing this as well as facing what seems the mysterious new technical world of computers can often be intimidating to the computer/internet newcomer.

Access to information and entertainment, credit and financial services, products from every corner of the world, even to your work, is greater than earlier generations could ever have imagined. Thanks to the Internet, you can order books, clothes, or appliances online; reserve a hotel room across the ocean; download music and games; check your bank balance 24 hours a day; talk to friends on the other side of the world; or access your workplace from thousands of miles away. The flip-side, however, is that the Internet, and the anonymity it affords, also can give online scammers, hackers, and identity thieves access to your computer, personal information, finances, and more. But with awareness as your safety net, you can minimize the chance of an Internet mishap. Being on guard online helps you protect your information, your computer, even yourself.

This book is intended to help you overcome the intimidation factor and introduce you to the basics of exploring and using the Internet safely. You will notice that there are references to the same dangers and preventions in various sections of this book. This is because they are essential to the subject and applicable to the remedy. For example; Privacy on the Internet is approached much like the subject of Security on the Internet; both are very important and are achieved in much the same way. This also makes it much easier for you to refer to this guide later to solve the problems particular to a specific section or subject.

We live in a fast changing world and computers and the Internet are no exception, and indeed they are often the cause or engine of these changes. But there are basic standards and protective methods that all Internet users should know which help them travel through cyberspace safely just as there are rules of the road on our neighborhood streets and national highways that keep us safe. Hopefully this book will guide you on a safe journey and prevent you from having to learn the hard way of the dangers and pitfalls that exists in the so-called virtual world. So just think of this book as your introductory *Internet Safety Manual* helping you along to the day when you become computer confident, well traveled and cyber-savy.

Welcome to Cyberspace.

The Connection;
How to Go Online

You hear about the Internet all the time, on the news, in conversations with other people, and in advertisements. But you're not sure about going online. What can it do for you? Is it safe? How do you get started?

This section will help answer these questions and give you the information you need to "make the connection" to the Internet. Following is a glossary included to help you understand some basic online terms. Refer to this glossary when needed as you progress through this guidebook.

Why Go Online?

You can save time and money, communicate with people quickly and easily, get information you need, and have fun on the Internet. Here are just some of the things you can do:

- Exchange messages, photos and documents with friends and family;

- Shop for all kinds of products and services, from airline tickets to antiques, rental cars to real estate;

- Keep track of your finances and pay bills;

- Plan trips, get maps, even find out what the weather will be at your destination;

- Buy and sell stocks;

- Contact government agencies and other sources of information and assistance;

- Get information and advice about health issues; and

- Discuss your hobbies or other topics with people who have the same interests as you.

Think of the Internet as a tool that you can use as much or as little as you want, any time, from anywhere. You can also learn how to do new things gradually, not being concerned about the necessity to be a computer expert. You don't even need your own equipment and Internet access; you may be able to go online free at your local library, school, or community center.

Is It Safe To Go Online?

Going online is a lot like going for a walk, using the telephone, or answering a knock on your door. The same common- sense precautions apply.

8 Common-Sense Online Safety Rules

(These will be discussed in depth later in the book)

1. Guard your online account numbers carefully so no one else can use them pretending to be you.

2. Don't give your address or other personal information to strangers you "chat" with online or who send you e-mail.

3. Don't believe promises of big profits, risk- free investments, easy credit, or valuable prizes.

4. Do business with companies and charities you know and trust, and check out unfamiliar ones with your local or state consumer protection agency and the Better Business Bureau.

5. Find out how personal information you may be asked to provide will be used, whether it will be shared with others, and how you can control its use.

6. Look for explanations about how your financial and other personal information is safeguarded when you send it and in storage, if it is kept at the other end.

7. Be wary of documents attached to e-mails from unknown sources or computer programs offered by unfamiliar Web sites; they may contain computer viruses.

8. Don't assume that the people you communicate with online are who they say they are; it's easy to mask your true identity on the Internet.

You'll find many easy-to-use online tools to help you protect your online privacy and security. For example, your own computer browser may show whether the information you're sending to a Web site is being securely transmitted. Special software can alert you to computer viruses. And there are many ways to control who tracks your movements on the Internet and determine if a Web site's privacy policy is satisfactory. Your Internet service provider (ISP) may be a good source of information and other resources are listed at the end of this book.

How Do I Get Started?

Most people go online using a computer with a modem, which is either built-in or a separate item. The modem plugs into the wall outlet for your telephone and dials a number to reach the service that you have chosen to connect you to the Internet. If you're going to be online a lot, consider getting a second phone line or ask your local or long distance telephone company about other options. For instance, new technology may allow you to connect by telephone without tying up your line.

Depending on the service that's available in your area, you may be able to connect to an Internet service provider (ISP) through your cable television wire or by satellite as an alternative to a telephone line. And instead of a computer, you could go online using equipment such as your television, a cellular phone, or some other wireless device. Technology is changing fast and there are more and more choices for how to go online, so take the time to explore all the possibilities.

No matter what you use to go online, your Internet service provider (ISP) is the gateway. Telephone and cable companies may provide this service, and there are many other companies to choose from as well. Some provide just the basics; e-mail and access to the Internet. Other providers offer extra benefits such as their own online shopping "malls, chat rooms, and customized services."

When you sign up (it takes special software and a modem), you'll be asked to enter a screen name, a secret password and your credit card number. Usually, online charges are billed to your credit card. Most providers allow you to review your monthly expenses online instead of sending you a separate itemized bill. If you note unexpected charges from your ISP, call for an explanation. If you're not satisfied with the explanation, or think you may be the victim of fraud, write a letter to your credit card company and your state Attorney General.

7 Things To Consider In Choosing Your Internet Service Provider (ISP)

1. Ask your friends and relatives what providers they use and if they're happy with the service they receive.

2. If you plan to connect through a phone line, choose a service that has a local number to dial in so you won't have to pay toll-charges while you're online.

3. Look for companies you can reach both online and offline (by a local or toll- free number) if you need help and that have customer service 24 hours a day, seven days a week.

4. Find out what features different providers offer and decide which are most important to you.

5. Compare prices. Some providers charge flat monthly fees; some charge by the minute; and others may give you a choice or combination of both. Some even provide free service, but you may have advertisements appear on your screen in exchange.

6. Know the provider's privacy policy. Find out what information is collected about you, how that information is used, and how you can control your personal information.

7. Pay attention to security. Find out how your personal information is protected from inappropriate access by others outside and inside the company.

Some Internet service providers (ISP) offer discounts if you sign up for a long- term contract and pay in advance. But things change quickly, and companies come and go. It may make more sense to sign up for service that gives you the flexibility to change to another provider easily if you choose.

Cyberspeak; Learning the Language

You don't have to be a computer expert to book a trip into Cyberspace, but it certainly helps to know a few words of cyber-speak. Before long, you'll sound like a native and get around like an experienced traveler. Below are many (but not all) of the basic online and computer terms that you will become familiar with as you become more experienced with your PC and the Internet. Refer to these terms as you progress through the book or need clarification when they are used.

Basic Online Terms

BOOKMARK — an online function that retains the address of and access to your favorite web sites quickly.

BROWSER — special software that allows you to navigate several areas of the Internet and view a web site. A computer program that helps you find your way around on the Internet.

BLOGGER — a person who writes blogs or weblogs. A website provides the tools for creating blogs (weblogs). After users select a pre-designed template or create one with their look and feel, every posting entered is published to the *blogger page* on the website automatically.

BULLETIN BOARD/NEWSGROUP — places to leave an electronic message or share news that anyone can read and respond to. Marketers or others can get your e-mail address from bulletin boards and newsgroups.

CHAT ROOM — a place for people to converse online by typing messages to each other. (Once you're in a chat room, others can contact you by e-mail. Some online services monitor their chat rooms and encourage children to report offensive chatter. Some allow parents to deny access to chat rooms altogether.)

CHATTING — a way for a group of people to converse online in real-time by typing messages to each other. Live discussions with people who gather at a particular place (called a chatroom) online and type messages that others who are there can read and respond to immediately.

COOKIE — a bit of electronic information that can be placed in your computer when you visit a Web site to track what you look at there, recognize you when you return, and in some cases, track where else you go on the Internet. when you visit a site, a notation may be fed to a file " known as a "cookie" in your computer for future reference. If you revisit the site, the "cookie" file allows the web site to identify you as a "return" guest and offer you products tailored to your interests or tastes. You can set your online preferences to limit or let you know about "cookies" that a web site places on your computer.

CYBERSPACE — another name for the Internet.

DOWNLOAD — the transfer of files or software from a remote computer to your computer. The opposite of *upload*.

E-MAIL — computer-to-computer messages between one or more individuals via the Internet. An electronic message that is typed and sent to a specific person or group of people.

ENCRYPTION — a method used to scramble information such as a credit card account number so it can be transmitted securely and unscrambled only by the person for whom it was intended.

FILTER — software you can buy that lets you block access to web sites and content that you may find unsuitable.

HACKER — a person who uses the Internet to access computers without permission.

HARDWARE — A computer, screen, keyboard, and other equipment.

INTERNET — the universal network that allows computers to talk to other computers in words, text, graphics, and sound, anywhere in the world. A global system that allows computers to communicate with each other.

ISP (Internet Service Provider) — a service that allows you to connect to the Internet. A company that provides access to the Internet and may also offer other online services to members or subscribers.

JUNK E-MAIL — unsolicited commercial e-mail; also known as "spam" or "junk mail." Usually junk e-mail doesn't contain the recipient's address on the "To" line. Instead, the addressee is a made-up name, such as "friend@public.com." Or the address on the "To" line is identical to the one on the "From' line.

KEYWORD — a word you enter into a search engine to begin the search for specific information or web sites.

LINKS — highlighted words (most often by underlining) on a web site that allow you to connect to other parts of the same web site or to other web sites.

LISTSERV — an online mailing list that allows individuals or organizations to send e-mail to groups of people at one time.

MODEM — an internal or external device that connects your computer to a phone line and, if you wish, to a company that can link you to the Internet.

NEWSGROUP — a place where you can post messages for others to read later.

ONLINE SERVICE — an ISP with added information, entertainment and shopping features.

PASSWORD — a personal code that you use to access your account with your ISP or other types of accounts you may have voluntarily subscribed to on the Internet.

PRIVACY POLICY — a statement on a web site describing what information about you the site collects, and how it is used. Ideally, the policy is posted prominently and offers you options about the use of your personal information. These options are called opt-in and opt-out. An opt-in choice means the web site won't use your information unless you specifically say it's okay. An opt-out choice means the web site can use the information unless you specifically direct it not to.

SCREEN NAME — the name you call yourself when you communicate online. You may want to abbreviate your name or make up a name. Your ISP may allow you to use several screen names.

SEARCH ENGINE — a function that lets you search for information and web sites. Using a search engine is like accessing the main card file in a library, only easier. A few keywords can lead you almost anywhere on the Internet. You can find search engines or a search function on many web sites.

SOFTWARE — a program that tells computers how to do specific things.

SPAM — unsolicited e-mail sometimes referred to as "junk e-mail" or "junk mail."

SPAMMER — someone who sends mass amounts of unsolicited commercial e-mail.

UPLOAD — the transfer of files or software from your computer to a remote computer. The opposite of *download*.

URL (Uniform Resource Locator) — the address that lets you locate a particular site. For example, http://www.ftc.gov is the URL for the Federal Trade Commission. All government URLs end in *.gov*. Non-profit organizations and trade associations end in *.org*. For example, http://www.naag.org is the URL for the National Association of Attorneys General. Commercial companies now end in *.com*, although additional suffixes or domains may be used as the number of businesses on the Internet grows. Other countries use different endings.

VIRUS — also known as "malicious programs" or "malicious software." It is a file maliciously planted in your computer that can disrupt your system. A computer code that can damage your files. Special software can warn about viruses and sometimes fix the damage they cause.

WEB SITE — (or *Site* for short) An Internet destination where you can look at and retrieve data. A place on the Internet that is made up of one or more "pages" and may be created by an individual, an organization, a government agency, a school, or a company to offer information and, in many cases, to allow interactive communication with visitors. All the web sites in the world, linked together, make up the World Wide Web or the "Web."

Site Seeing
On The Internet

The Savvy Cyber Traveler

Millions of people are traveling the Internet (a.k.a. Cyberspace). And as going online gets easier and more affordable, even more will venture into Cyberspace.

Because Cyberspace is an image on a computer screen, sometimes it is called a "virtual" world; not actually real. But travel anywhere has real risks and rewards. No matter where you go, even if you don't actually leave your home to get there, common sense and knowledge are your best travel companions

Getting the Most From Your Travel

There is so much to do in Cyberspace and so many "sites" to see that you may wish you had a tour guide. Chances are your Internet service provider (ISP) offers a lot of information on its web site; from news to shopping to games; including links to other web sites. If you know where you want to go, you can simply type in the URL and go there. Or, you can use a search engine to look among web sites to find what you're looking for.

Travel Tip:

A little planning goes a long way on the Internet. Try to identify the sites you want to visit or determine the subject areas you're interested in learning more about. It will help you save time, and if you pay for your online service by the hour, it will keep your charges under control.

You might visit a famous museum, catch the latest news, enter a *chat room* to discuss a topic that interests you, learn about parenting, search for a travel bargain, purchase a book or CD, start a part-time business, or *e-mail* a letter to your far-flung family in a single step.

Books, articles, friends, and people you work with can steer you to many interesting *web sites*. Once you're on the road, your own curiosity and interests will lead you to even more sites.

Information; The Currency of Cyberspace

When you enter Cyberspace, you've arrived in a global marketplace stocked with products and services. But the Internet's major currency is information. You seek it from others. Others seek it from you. Marketers, in particular, want to know as much about you and your buying habits as you are willing to tell. Since some information may be quite personal, you'll want to know how it is gathered, how it is used, and occasionally abused. Just as you might carry cash in a secret pouch when you go abroad, you may want to protect certain information when you go online.

Travel Tip:

> When you enter a web site look for a privacy policy that answers your questions about accuracy, access, security, and control of personal information, as well as how information will be used, and whether it will be provided to third parties.

Information is gathered on the Internet both directly and indirectly. When you enter a chat room discussion, leave a message on a bulletin board, register with a commercial site, enter a contest, or order a product, you directly and knowingly send information into Cyberspace. Often, a web site may require information from you as the "toll" you pay to enter.

Data also can be gathered indirectly, without your knowledge. For example, your travels around a web site can be tracked by a file called a "cookie" left on your computer's hard drive on your first visit to that site. When you revisit the site, it will open the cookie file and access the stored information so it will know how to greet you. You may even be welcomed by name. If you linger over a product or a subject that interests you, it will be noted. And soon, you may see ads on the site that look as if they've been custom tailored for you. As web sites gather information directly and indirectly, they can collect a complete data picture of you and your family. This kind of information is valuable to marketers because it helps them target their sales efforts.

Maintaining Privacy When You Travel The Net

It's difficult to be anonymous once you've ventured into Cyberspace. Expect to receive unsolicited advertising e-mail, even personalized ads that seem to know you. This so-called junk e-mail can be a nuisance, even a scam. If it looks questionable, simply delete it. Check with your ISP or online service for ways to limit unsolicited e-mail. This will also be covered in depth later in the book.

As anywhere, Cyberspace has its share of "snoopers" and con men. Guard your password. It's the key to your account. People who work for your service provider should never request your password. If they do, refuse the request and report the incident to your service provider immediately.

Travel Tip:

> Know who you're "talking" to. Don't give out personal information to strangers.

When shopping online, be very careful about revealing your Social Security or credit card number and shipping address. Many web sites scramble or encrypt information like that to ensure the safety of your personal data. Look at the privacy policy for information about how the web sites you visit scramble or encrypt your personal data. This technology is improving rapidly, but still is not foolproof.

Concerns about loss of privacy are not new. But the computer's ability to gather and sort vast amounts of data and the Internet's ability to distribute it globally magnify those concerns.

To a large extent, privacy is up to you when you enter a web site. Look for a privacy statement. Sites that are most sensitive to your privacy concerns not only have privacy policies, but also display them clearly and conspicuously, offer you a choice to share your personal information or restrict its use, and explain how your information will be used.

Travel Insurance For Cyberspace

Experienced cyber travelers carry a little "travel insurance" when they enter Cyberspace. Here are some tips from the experts:

- Don't give out your account password to anyone, even someone claiming to be from your online service. Your account can be hijacked, and you can find unexpected charges on your bill.
- People aren't always who they seem to be in Cyberspace. Be careful about giving out your credit card number. The same applies to your Social Security number, phone number and home address.
- Be aware that when you enter a chat room, others can know you are there and can even e-mail you once you start chatting. To remain anonymous, you may want to use a nickname for your screen name.
- E-mail is relatively private — *but not completely.* Don't put anything into an electronic message that you wouldn't want to see posted on a neighborhood bulletin board.
- Check your online service for ways to reduce unsolicited commercial e-mail. Learn to recognize junk e-mail, and delete it. Don't even read it first. Never download an e-mail attachment from an

      unknown source. Opening a file could expose your
      system to a virus.

- You can be defrauded online. If an offer is too hard to believe, don't believe it.
- Credit rights and other consumer protection laws apply to Internet transactions. If you have a problem, tell a law enforcement agency.
- Teach your children to check with you before giving out personal or family information and to look for privacy policies when they enter a web site that asks for information about them. Many kids' sites now insist on a parent's approval before they gather information from a child. Still, some openly admit they will use the information any way they please.

Traveling With Children

Taking the kids on a trip into Cyberspace can be a rewarding experience for you as well as your children. Before embarking on your trip, you should know that web sites collect a significant amount of personal information from children, such as the child's name, postal and e-mail address, and favorite activities and products. This information can be collected by asking children to register with the site, join a kids' club, enter a contest or complete a questionnaire online.

The personal information collected is used to create customer lists. In some cases, these are sold to list brokers, who, in turn, rent the lists to other advertisers. (Often, this practice is not revealed. Look at a web site's privacy policy for an explanation of how the site handles your personal information.) Sometimes this information is posted on the web site in "guest books," members' profiles, chat rooms or on home pages hosted by a web site. Posting such information may enable others to contact your child, possibly without your knowledge. It's unlikely that you'd let personal information about your child be posted on a neighborhood bulletin board; exercise the same caution with electronic bulletin boards.

Children learn to use computers quickly, but because they lack life experience, they can reveal information you might not wish to share. That's one reason children should be supervised when they venture into Cyberspace. Here are some precautions you may want to take:

- Explore the Internet with your children. It's the best way to see what they see online. There are plenty of kid-friendly sites; help your kids find them, and explain why it's best to be careful not to give out their real name and address in chat rooms, to online pen pals and on bulletin boards.
- Consider using filters that allow you to place certain sites and subjects off limits to your child. These "parent controls" are available through your online service or through special software you can buy. Filters aren't foolproof, but they help. Some ISPs offer filters to control the amount of unsolicited e-mail you receive.
- Have rules for going online. When your child has earned the right, issue a Cyberspace Passport and post it as a reminder of the achievement.
- Teach your children the meaning of privacy and personal or family information. Encourage them to post messages only with your permission and supervision.

- Show your child the difference between an advertisement and entertainment. A young child may not realize that an animated or cartoon character may be gathering market data or trying to sell something.

Rules of the "Virtual" Road

Children are exceptionally vulnerable on the Internet and are all too often the object of predators and scam artist of all types. One of the best ways to protect your children is to be sure they understand the risk and dangers and always show you are maintaining an interest in where they are going and what they are doing on the internet. Like a news reporter, parents should know the WHO, WHAT, WHERE, WHEN, and WHY of their child's Internet experience. Those same five Ws that rule the curiosities of the news reporter when used by a parent can help keep a child traveling safely and on the right side of the cyberspace super highway.

Children act more responsibly when they know the rules. That's why you may find the idea of a parent-child contract helpful when it comes to using the Web. Here are some rules of the "virtual" road, along with a sample Cyberspace Passport for children who accept the rules. You and your children may want to develop others.

Cyberspace Passport

These rules are for my safety. I will honor them when I go online.

I can go online

_____ (Time of day) for _____ (How long)

It is ___ *OK* ___ *Not OK* for me to go online without a parent.

I understand which sites I can visit and which ones are off limits.

I won't give out information about my family or myself without permission from my parents.

My password is my secret. I won't give it to anyone.

I will never agree to meet an online pal, or send my picture, without permission from my parents.

I know an advertisement when I see one. I also know that animated or cartoon characters aren't real and may be trying to sell me something or to get information from me.

I will follow these same rules when I am at home, in school, or at the library or a friend's.

Privacy on the Internet

Technology now provides companies with the ability to collect information about you and potentially give that information to others. While the Internet can serve as a tremendous resource for information, products and services, you should be sure to safeguard your privacy online by following these tips.

Protect your personal information. It's valuable

Why? To an identity thief, your personal information can provide instant access to your financial accounts, your credit record, and other assets.

If you think no one would be interested in your personal information, think again. The reality is that anyone can be a victim of identity theft. In fact, according to a Federal Trade Commission (FTC) survey, there are almost 10 million victims a year. It's often difficult to know how thieves obtained their victims' personal information, and while it definitely can happen offline, some cases start when online data is stolen. Visit *http://www.ftc.gov/bcp/edu/microsites/idtheft//* to learn what to do if your identity is stolen.

Unfortunately, when it comes to crimes like identity theft, you can't entirely control whether you will become a victim. But following these tips can help minimize your risk while you're online:

- If you're asked for your personal information— your name, e-mail or home address, phone number, account numbers, or Social Security number—find out how it's going to be used and how it will be protected before you share it. If you have children, teach them to not give out your last name, your home address, or your phone number on the Internet.
- If you get an e-mail or pop-up message asking for personal information, don't reply or click on the link in the message. The safest course of action is not to respond to requests for your personal or financial information. If you believe there may be a need for such information by a company with whom you have an account or placed an order, contact that company directly in a way you know to be genuine. In any case, don't send your personal information via e-mail because e-mail is not a secure transmission method.
- If you are shopping online, don't provide your personal or financial information through a company's website until you have checked for indicators that the site is secure, like a lock icon on the browser's status bar or a website URL that begins "https:" (the "s" stands for "secure"). Unfortunately, no indicator is foolproof; some scammers have forged security icons.
- Read website privacy policies. They should explain what personal information the website collects, how the information is used, and whether it is provided to third parties. The privacy policy also should tell you whether you have the right to see what information the website has about you and what security measures the company takes to protect your information. If you don't see a privacy policy or if you can't understand it consider doing business elsewhere.

Reminder

A hacker is a person who uses the Internet to access computers without permission. A spammer is someone who sends mass amounts of unsolicited commercial e-mail. A virus is software that spreads from computer to computer and damages files or disrupts your system.

EASY AS ABC

When exploring online, think ABC to remember the privacy and security questions you should ask about a company.

> **About me.** What information does the company collect about me and is it secure?

> **Benefits.** How does the company use that information and what is the benefit to me?

> **Choices.** What choices do I have about the company's use of information about me? Can I opt out of the information uses and how?

Make choices

Many companies give you a choice on their Web site as to whether and how your personal information is used. These companies allow you to decline or "opt-out" of having personal information, such as your e-mail address, used or shared with other companies. Look for this as part of the company's privacy policy.

Security on the Internet

The Internet is an exciting tool that puts vast information at your fingertips. With a click of a mouse, it lets you buy an airline ticket, book a hotel, send flowers to a friend, or purchase your favorite stock.

Good deals, convenience and choices abound on the Internet. But before you use all the Internet has to offer, be cyber smart and make your online experience safe.

Shopping online offers lots of benefits that you won't find shopping in a store or by mail. For example, the Internet is always open - seven days a week, 24 hours a day. And, bargains can be numerous online. Shopping on the Internet also can be as safe as shopping in a store or by mail. Keep in mind the following tips to help ensure that your online shopping experience is a safe one.

Use a secure browser

This is the software you use to navigate the Internet. Your browser should comply with industry security standards, such as Secure Sockets Layer (SSL) or SET Secure Electronic Transaction. These standards encrypt or scramble the purchase information you send over the Internet, ensuring the security of your transaction. Most computers come with a browser already installed. You also can download some browsers for free over the Internet.

Be sure to set up your operating system and Web browser software properly, and update them regularly. Hackers also take advantage of Web browsers (like Internet Explorer or Netscape) and operating system software (like Windows or Linux) that are unsecured. Lessen your risk by changing the settings in your browser or operating system and increasing your online security. Check the "Tools" or "Options" menus for built-in security features. If you need help understanding your choices, use your "Help" function.

Your operating system also may offer free software "patches" or "security updates" that close holes in the system that hackers could exploit. In fact, some common operating systems can be set to automatically retrieve and install patches for you. If your system does not do this, bookmark the website for your system's manufacturer so you can regularly visit and update your system with defenses against the latest attacks. Updating can be as simple as one click. Your e-mail software may help you avoid viruses by giving you the ability to filter certain types of spam. It's up to you to activate the filter.

If you're not using your computer for an extended period, turn it off or unplug it from the phone or cable line. When it's off, the computer doesn't send or receive information from the Internet and isn't vulnerable to hackers.

Know who you're dealing with

And know what you're getting into. There are dishonest people in the bricks and mortar world and on the Internet. Anyone can set up shop online under almost any name. But online, you can't judge an operator's trustworthiness with a gut-affirming look in the eye. It's remarkably simple for online scammers to impersonate a legitimate business, so you need to know who you're dealing with. If you're shopping online, check out the seller before you buy. If you're not familiar with a merchant, ask for a paper catalog or brochure to get a better idea of their merchandise and services. A legitimate business or individual seller should give you a physical address and a working telephone number at which they can be contacted in case you have problems. Also, determine the company's refund and return policies before you place your order.

Keep your password(s) private

Protect your passwords. Keep your passwords in a secure place, and out of plain view. Don't share your passwords on the Internet, over e-mail, or on the phone. Your Internet Service Provider (ISP) should never ask for your password. In addition, hackers may try to figure out your passwords to gain access to your computer. You can make it tougher for them by:

- Using passwords that have at least eight characters and include numbers or symbols.
- Avoiding common words: some hackers use programs that can try every word in the dictionary.
- Not using your personal information, your login name, or adjacent keys on the keyboard as passwords.
- Changing your passwords regularly (at a minimum, every 90 days).
- Not using the same password for each online account you access.

One way to create a strong password is to think of a memorable phrase and use the first letter of each word as your password, converting some letters into numbers that resemble letters. For example,"How much wood could a woodchuck chuck" would become HmWc@wcC.

Be creative when you establish a password, and never give it to anyone. Avoid using a telephone number, birth date, or a portion of your Social Security number. Instead, use a combination of numbers, letters, and symbols.

Pay by credit or charge card

If you pay by credit or charge card online, your transaction will be protected by the Fair Credit Billing Act. Under this law, consumers have the right to dispute charges under certain circumstances and temporarily withhold payment while the creditor is investigating them. In the case of unauthorized use of a consumer's credit or charge card, consumers are generally held liable only for the first $50 in charges. Some cards may provide additional warranty or purchase protection benefits.

PHISHING - Bait or Prey?

"We suspect an unauthorized transaction on your account. To ensure that your account is not compromised, please click the link below and confirm your identity."

This is an example of the often used words of "Phishers" who send spam or pop-up messages claiming to be from a business or organization that you might deal with—for example it could be an Internet service provider (ISP), bank, online payment service, or even a government agency. The message usually says that you need to "update" or "validate" your account information. It might threaten some dire consequence if you don't respond. The message directs you to a website that looks just like a legitimate organization's, but isn't. The purpose of the bogus site? To trick you into divulging your personal information so the operators can steal your identity and run up bills or commit crimes in your name. Don't take the bait: never reply to or click on links in e-mail or pop-ups that ask for personal information.

Legitimate companies don't ask for this information via e-mail. If you are directed to a website to update your information, verify that the site is legitimate by calling the company directly, using contact information from your account statements. Or open a new browser window and type the URL into the address field, watching that the actual URL of the site you visit doesn't change and is still the one you intended to visit. Forward spam that is phishing for information to *spam@uce.gov* and to the company, bank, or organization impersonated in the phishing e-mail. Most organizations have information on their websites about where to report problems.

Keep a record

Be sure to print a copy of your purchase order and confirmation number for your records. Also, you should know that the federal Mail or Telephone Order Merchandise Rule covers orders made via the Internet. This means that unless stated otherwise, merchandise must be delivered within 30 days, and if there are delays, the company must notify you.

Pay your bills online

Some companies let you pay bills and check your account status online. Before you sign up for any service, evaluate how the company is securing your financial and personal information. Many companies explain their security procedures on their Web site. If you don't see a security description, call or e-mail the company and ask.

Online Security & Safety Tips

As we all come to enjoy and rely upon the Internet to learn, work and play we should always remember that the same qualities that make the online world so enriching can also make us more vulnerable to criminal hackers who seek to do harm.

Just as you take precautions to keep your home safe from burglars, there are steps you can take to help protect your personal computer (PC) and yourself from cyber criminals.

Here is a reminder of the three steps you can take to make your computer more secure:

      1. Use an Internet firewall

      2. Get computer updates

      3. Use up-to-date anti-virus software

Use an Internet firewall

A firewall is software that helps create a protective barrier between your computer and potentially harmful attacks. Many businesses have firewalls built into their networks, but home users should install firewall software if it was not included in the software package that came with their PC.

Don't be put off by the word "firewall." It's not necessary to fully understand how it works; it's enough to know what it does and why you need it. Firewalls help keep hackers from using your computer to send out your personal information without your permission. While anti-virus software scans incoming e-mail and files, a firewall is like a guard, watching for outside attempts to access your system and blocking communications to and from sources you don't permit. Some operating systems and hardware devices come with a built-in firewall that may be shipped in the "off" mode. Make sure you turn it on. For your firewall to be effective, it needs to be set up properly and updated regularly. Check your online "Help" feature for specific instructions.
If your operating system doesn't include a firewall, get a separate software firewall that runs in the background while you work, or install a hardware firewall—an external device that includes firewall software. Several free firewall software programs are available on the Internet.

ZOMBIE DRONES - Some spammers search the Internet for unprotected computers they can control and use anonymously to send unwanted spam e-mails. If you don't have up-to-date anti-virus protection and a firewall, spammers may try to install software that lets them route e-mail through your computer, often to thousands of recipients, so that it appears to have come from your account. If this happens, you may receive an overwhelming number of complaints from recipients, and your e-mail account could be shut down by your Internet Service Provider (ISP).

Even with the protection of a firewall, it's smart to back up your files on a regular basis to protect them in case your system does get damaged. Copy your important documents and files onto a floppy disk, CD or flash drive for safekeeping.

Get computer updates

No matter what software you use, you need to make sure your computer is protected by installing the latest security updates. Security updates help shield your computer from viruses, worms and other threats as they are discovered.

Check your software maker's Web site for new security updates or use the automated updating features that some companies offer.

Use anti-virus software

Anti-virus software protects your computer from viruses that can destroy your data, slow your computer's performance, cause a crash, or even allow spammers to send e-mail through your account. It works by scanning your computer and your incoming e-mail for viruses, and then deleting them. To be effective, your anti-virus software should update routinely with antidotes to the latest "bugs" circulating through the Internet. Most commercial anti-virus software includes a feature to download updates automatically when you are on the Internet.

Viruses, worms and other forms of malicious code pose a real threat to your computer, so you need to help defend it by using anti-virus software. New viruses and worms are emerging all the time; so anti-virus programs need regular updates so they can recognize the new threats. The more often your anti-virus software is updated the better. Sign up for regular updates from your anti-virus software company.

Dealing with anti-virus and firewall protection may sound about as exciting as flossing your teeth, but it's just as important as a preventive measure. Having intense dental treatment is never fun; neither is dealing with the effects of a preventable computer virus.

Anti-virus software
What to Look For and Where to Get It

You can download anti-virus software from the websites of software companies or buy it in retail stores. Look for anti-virus software that:

- Recognizes current viruses, as well as older ones.
- Effectively reverses the damage.
- Updates automatically.

Free software and file-sharing
WORTH THE HIDDEN COSTS?

Every day, millions of computer users share files online. File-sharing can give people access to a wealth of information, including music, games, and software. How does it work? You download special software that connects your computer to an informal network of other computers running the same software. Millions of users could be connected to each other through this software at one time. Often the software is free and easily accessible.

But file-sharing can have a number of risks. If you don't check the proper settings, you could allow access not just to the files you intend to share, but also to other information on your hard drive, like your tax returns, e-mail messages, medical records, photos, or other personal documents. In addition, you may unwittingly download pornography labeled as something else. Or you may download material that is protected by the copyright laws, which would mean you could be breaking the law. If you decide to use file-sharing software, set it up very carefully. Take the time to read the End User License Agreement to be sure you understand the side effects of any free downloads.

Spyware

Many free downloads, whether from peers or businesses, come with potentially undesirable side effects. Spyware is software installed without your knowledge or consent that adversely affects your ability to use your computer, sometimes by monitoring or controlling how you use it. To avoid spyware, resist the urge to install any software unless you know exactly what it is. Your anti-virus software may include anti-spyware capability that you can activate, but if it doesn't, you can install separate anti-spyware software, and then use it regularly to scan for and delete any spyware programs that may sneak onto your computer.

E-mail attachments and links
LEGITIMATE or VIRUS-LADEN?

Most viruses sent over e-mail or Instant Messenger won't damage your computer without your participation. For example, you would have to open an e-mail or attachment that includes a virus or follow a link to a site that is programmed to infect your computer. So hackers often lie to get you to open the e-mail attachment or click on a link. Some virus-laden e-mails appear to come from a friend or colleague; some have an appealing file name, like "Fwd: FUNNY" or "Per your request!" Others promise to clean a virus off your computer if you open it or follow the link. Don't open an e-mail attachment even if it appears to be from a friend or coworker unless you are expecting it or know what it contains. You can help others trust your attachments by including a message in your text explaining what you're attaching.

Following are a few other general tips to help avoid online threats such as spam, spyware, identity theft and inappropriate content.

Other online safety tips

- Protect your information by using a hard to guess password that is at least eight characters long and contains a mixture of letters, numbers and symbols.
- Reduce spam by only giving out your e-mail address to people you know and by never replying to spam - not even to unsubscribe.
- Be careful about opening attachments to e-mails, as they are one of the main ways viruses are spread from computer to computer.
- Be wary of any e-mail asking for personal information; for example, check to make sure a charity is legitimate before responding to an e-mail solicitation for donations.
- If you have kids that use your computer, consider using parental control software that helps you choose what they see on the Internet.
- To help prevent spyware from being installed on your computer, read the installation agreements carefully when you download from the Internet. If you find you already have it on your system, there are anti-spyware tools available to remove it.

Backup important files - If you follow these tips, you're more likely to be more secure online, free of interference from hackers, viruses, and spammers. But no system is completely secure. If you have important files stored on your computer, copy them onto a removable device, and store them in a safe place.

Working together

Learn who to contact if something goes wrong online.

Hacking or Computer Virus - If your computer gets hacked or infected by a virus:

- Immediately unplug the phone or cable line from your machine. Then scan your entire computer with fully updated anti-virus software, and update your firewall.
- Take steps to minimize the chances of another incident.
- Alert the appropriate authorities by contacting
  - o your ISP and the hacker's ISP (if you can tell what it is). You can usually find an ISP's e-mail address on its website. Include information on the incident from your firewall's log file. By alerting the ISP to the problem on its system, you can help it prevent similar problems in the future.
  - o the FBI at *http://www.ic3.gov/*. To fight computer criminals, they need to hear from you.

Internet Fraud - If a scammer takes advantage of you through an Internet auction, when you're shopping online, or in any other way, report it to the Federal Trade Commission, at *www.ftc.gov*. The FTC enters Internet, identity theft, and other fraud-related complaints into Consumer Sentinel, a secure, online database available to hundreds of civil and criminal law enforcement agencies in the U.S. and abroad.

Deceptive Spam - If you get deceptive spam, including e-mail phishing for your information, forward it to *spam@uce.gov*. Be sure to include the full header of the e-mail, including all routing information.

Divulged Personal Information - If you believe you have mistakenly given your personal information to a fraudster, file a complaint at *www.ftc.gov*, and then visit the Federal Trade Commission's Identity Theft website at *http://www.ftc.gov/bcp/edu/microsites/idtheft//* to learn how to minimize your risk of damage from a potential theft of your identity.

PARENTS

Parental controls are provided by most ISPs, or are sold as separate software. Remember that no software can substitute for parental supervision. Talk to your kids about safe computing practices, as well as the things they're seeing and doing online.

Keeping safe from cyber criminals is a top priority because there is no single solution to prevent cyber attacks. Developing improved technology, partnering with industry peers to increase public awareness, supporting law enforcement efforts to bring cyber criminals to justice, and working with lawmakers to develop effective policies contribute to a safer internet. Support the National Cyber Security Alliance, which does much to help consumers stay safe online through their Web site *www.staysafeonline.info*.

By using the safety tips in this guide, you too are playing a vital part to secure not only your own system but the broader computing environment as well

If all of us, industry, government and consumers, do our part, we can look forward to a more secure computing experience

BEWARE THE DOTCONS!

Dot com. Dot gov. Dot net. Dot org. Dot edu. Dot mil. Dot tv. The Internet has spawned a whole new lexicon and brought the world to your living room, 24/7/365. And while the opportunities online for consumers are almost endless, there are some challenges, too. As in the *dot con!*

Con artists have gone high-tech, using the Internet to defraud consumers in a variety of clever ways. Whether they're using the excitement of an Internet auction to entice consumers into parting with their money, applying new technology to peddle traditional business opportunity scams, using e-mail to reach vast numbers of people with false promises about earnings through day trading, or hijacking consumers' modems and cramming hefty long-distance charges onto their phone bills, scam artists are just a click away.

Fortunately, law enforcement is on the cyber-case. Using complaints to Consumer Sentinel, a consumer fraud database, as their guide, law enforcement officials have identified the top 10 dot cons facing consumers who surf the Internet, as well as many of the fraudsters behind them. In addition to putting many online con artists out of business, the Federal Trade Commission, the nation's chief consumer protection agency, wants consumers to know how not to get caught in their web.

According to the FTC, here's what online consumers are complaining about most:

Internet Auctions

The Bait: Shop in a "virtual marketplace" that offers a huge selection of products at great deals.
The Catch: After sending their money, consumers say they've received an item that is less valuable than promised, or, worse yet, nothing at all.
The Safety Net: When bidding through an Internet auction, particularly for a valuable item, check out the seller and insist on paying with a credit card or using an escrow service.

Internet Access Services

The Bait: Free money, simply for cashing a check.
The Catch: Consumers say they've been "trapped" into long-term contracts for Internet access or another web service, with big penalties for cancellation or early termination.
The Safety Net: If a check arrives at your home or business, read both sides carefully and look inside the envelope to find the conditions you're agreeing to if you cash the check. Read

your phone bill carefully for unexpected or unauthorized charges.

Credit Card Fraud

The Bait: Surf the Internet and view adult images online for free, just for sharing your credit card number to prove you're over 18.

The Catch: Consumers say that fraudulent promoters have used their credit card numbers to run up charges on their cards.

The Safety Net: Share credit card information only when buying from a company you trust. Dispute unauthorized charges on your credit card bill by complaining to the bank that issued the card. Federal law limits your liability to $50 in charges if your card is misused.

International Modem Dialing

The Bait: Get free access to adult material and pornography by downloading a "viewer" or "dialer" computer program.

The Catch: Consumers complained about exorbitant long-distance charges on their phone bill. Through the program, their modem is disconnected, and then reconnected to the Internet through an international long-distance number.

The Safety Net: Don't download any program to access a so-called "free" service without reading all the disclosures carefully for cost information. Just as important, read your phone bill carefully and challenge any charges you didn't authorize or don't understand.

Web Cramming

The Bait: Get a free custom-designed website for a 30-day trial period, with no obligation to continue.

The Catch: Consumers say they've been charged on their telephone bills or received a separate invoice, even if they never accepted the offer or agreed to continue the service after the trial period.

The Safety Net: Review your telephone bills and challenge any charges you don't recognize.

Multilevel Marketing Plans/ Pyramids

The Bait: Make money through the products and services you sell as well as those sold by the people you recruit into the program.

The Catch: Consumers say that they've bought into plans and programs, but their customers are other distributors, not the general public. Some multi-level marketing programs are actually illegal pyramid schemes. When products or services are sold only to distributors like you, there's no way to make money.

The Safety Net: Avoid plans that require you to recruit distributors, buy expensive inventory or commit to a minimum sales volume.

Travel and Vacation

The Bait: Get a luxurious trip with lots of "extras" at a bargain-basement price.

The Catch: Consumers say some companies deliver lower-quality accommodations and services than they've advertised or no trip at all. Others have been hit with hidden charges or additional requirements after they've paid.

The Safety Net: Get references on any travel company you're planning to do business with. Then, get details of the trip in writing, including the cancellation policy, before signing on.

Business Opportunities

The Bait: Be your own boss and earn big bucks.

The Catch: Taken in by promises about potential earnings, many consumers have invested in a "biz op" that turned out to be a "biz flop." There was no evidence to back up the earnings claims.

The Safety Net: Talk to other people who started businesses through the same company, get all the promises in writing, and study the proposed contract carefully before signing. Get an attorney or an accountant to take a look at it, too.

Investments

The Bait: Make an initial investment in a day trading system or service and you'll quickly realize huge returns.

The Catch: Big profits always mean big risk. Consumers have lost money to programs that claim to be able to predict the market with 100 percent accuracy.

The Safety Net: Check out the promoter with state and federal securities and commodities regulators, and talk to other people who invested through the program to find out what level of risk you're assuming.

Health Care Products/Services

The Bait: Items not sold through traditional suppliers are "proven" to cure serious and even fatal health problems.
The Catch: Claims for "miracle" products and treatments convince consumers that their health problems can be cured. But people with serious illnesses who put their hopes in these offers might delay getting the health care they need.
The Safety Net: Consult a health care professional before buying any "cure-all" that claims to treat a wide range of ailments or offers quick cures and easy solutions to serious illnesses.

Can you avoid getting caught by a scam artist working the web? Not always. But prudence pays. The FTC offers these tips to help you avoid getting caught by an offer that just may not click:

TIPS

- Be wary of extravagant claims about performance or earnings potential. Get all promises in writing and review them carefully before making a payment or signing a contract.
- Read the fine print and all relevant links. Fraudulent promoters sometimes bury the disclosures they're not anxious to share by putting them in teeny-tiny type or in a place where you're unlikely see them.
- Look for a privacy policy. If you don't see one - or if you can't understand it - consider taking your business elsewhere.

- Be skeptical of any company that doesn't clearly state its name, street address and telephone number. Check it out with the local Better Business Bureau, consumer protection office or state Attorney General.

Fraud: Avoiding Internet Investment Scams

The Internet serves as an excellent tool for investors, allowing them to easily and inexpensively research investment opportunities. But the Internet is also an excellent tool for fraudsters. That's why you should always think twice *before* you invest your money in any opportunity you learn about through the Internet.

This section tells you how to spot different types of Internet fraud, what the SEC is doing to fight Internet investment scams, and how to use the Internet to invest wisely.

Navigating the Frontier: Where the Frauds Are

The Internet allows individuals or companies to communicate with a large audience without spending a lot of time, effort, or money. Anyone can reach tens of thousands of people by building an Internet web site, posting a message on an online bulletin board, entering a discussion in a live "chat" room, or sending mass e-mails. It's easy for fraudsters to make their messages look real and credible. But it's nearly impossible for investors to tell the difference between fact and fiction.

Online Investment Newsletters

Hundreds of online investment newsletters have appeared on the Internet in recent years. Many offer investors seemingly unbiased information free of charge about featured companies or recommending "stock picks of the month." While legitimate online newsletters can help investors gather valuable information, some online newsletters are tools for fraud.

Some companies pay the people who write online newsletters cash or securities to "tout" or recommend their stocks. While this isn't illegal, the federal securities laws require the newsletters to disclose who paid them, the amount, and the type of payment. But many fraudsters fail to do so. Instead, they'll lie about the payments they received, their independence, their so-called research, and their track records. Their newsletters masquerade as sources of unbiased information, when in fact they stand to profit handsomely if they convince investors to buy or sell particular stocks.

Some online newsletters falsely claim to independently research the stocks they profile. Others spread false information or promote worthless stocks. The most notorious sometimes "scalp" the stocks they hype, driving up the price of the stock with their baseless recommendations and then selling their own holdings at high prices and high profits.

Bulletin Boards

Online bulletin boards, whether newsgroups, usenet, or web-based bulletin boards, have become an increasingly popular forum for investors to share information. Bulletin boards typically feature "threads" made up of numerous messages on various investment opportunities.

While some messages may be true, many turn out to be bogus or even scams. Fraudsters often pump up a company or pretend to reveal "inside" information about upcoming announcements, new products, or lucrative contracts
.
Also, you never know for certain who you're dealing with or whether they're credible because many bulletin boards allow users to hide their identity behind multiple aliases. People claiming to be unbiased observers who've carefully researched the company may actually be company insiders, large shareholders, or paid promoters. A single person can easily create the illusion of widespread interest in a small, thinly-traded stock by posting a series of messages under various aliases.

E-mail Spams

Because "spam" (junk e-mail) is so cheap and easy to create, fraudsters increasingly use it to find investors for bogus investment schemes or to spread false information about a company. Spam allows the unscrupulous to target many more potential investors than cold calling or mass mailing. Using a bulk e-mail program, spammers can send personalized messages to thousands and even millions of Internet users at a time.

Using the Internet to Invest Wisely

If you want to invest wisely and steer clear of frauds, you must get the facts. Never, ever, make an investment based solely on what you read in an online newsletter or bulletin board posting, especially if the investment involves a small, thinly-traded company that isn't well known. And don't even think about investing on your own in small companies that don't file regular reports with the SEC, unless you are willing to investigate each company thoroughly and to check the truth of every statement about the company. For instance, you'll need to:

- Get financial statements from the company and be able to analyze them;
- Verify the claims about new product developments or lucrative contracts;
- Call every supplier or customer of the company and ask if they really do business with the company; and
- Check out the people running the company and find out if they've ever made money for investors before.

And it doesn't stop there. Always watch out for tell-tale signs of fraud. Here's how you can use the Internet to help you invest wisely:

Start With the SEC's EDGAR Database

The federal securities laws require many public companies to register with the SEC and file annual reports containing audited financial statements. For example, the following companies must file reports with the SEC:

> - All U.S. companies with more than 500 investors *and* $10 million in net assets; and
> - All companies that list their securities on The Nasdaq Stock Market or a major national stock exchange such as the New York Stock Exchange.
> - Anyone can access and download these reports from the SEC's EDGAR database for free. Before you invest in a company, check to see whether it's registered with the SEC and read its reports.

But some companies don't have to register their securities or file reports on EDGAR. For example, companies raising less than $5 million in a 12-month period may be exempt from registering the transaction under a rule known as "Regulation A." Instead, these companies must file a hard copy of the "offering circular" with the SEC, containing financial statements and other information. Also, smaller companies raising less than one million dollars don't have to register with the SEC, but they must file a "Form D." Form D is a brief notice that includes the names and addresses of owners and stock promoters, but little other information. If you can't find a company on EDGAR, call the SEC at (202) 551-8090 to find out if the company filed an offering circular under Regulation A or a Form D. And be sure to request a copy.

The difference between investing in companies that register with the SEC and those that don't is like the difference between driving on a clear sunny day and driving at night without your headlights. You're asking for serious losses if you invest in small, thinly-traded companies that aren't widely known just by following the signs you read on Internet bulletin boards or online newsletters.

Contact Your State Securities Regulators

Don't stop with the SEC. You should always check with your state securities regulator, which you can find on the website of the North American Securities Administrators Association, to see if they have more information about the company and the people behind it. They can check the Central Registration Depository (CRD) and tell you whether the broker touting the stock or the broker's firm has a disciplinary history. They can also tell you whether they've cleared the offering for sale in your state.

Check with the Financial Industry Regulatory Authority (FINRA)

To check the disciplinary history of the broker or firm that's touting the stock, use FINRA's BrokerCheck website, or call FINRA's Broker Check Program hotline at (800) 289-9999.

Online Investment Fraud:
New Medium, Same Old Scam

The types of investment fraud seen online mirror the frauds perpetrated over the phone or through the mail. Remember that fraudsters can use a variety of Internet tools to spread false information, including bulletin boards, online newsletters, spam, or chat (including Internet Relay Chat or Web Page Chat). They can also build a glitzy, sophisticated web page. All of these tools cost very little money and can be found at the fingertips of fraudsters.

<u>Consider all offers with skepticism. Investment frauds usually fit one of the following categories:</u>

The "Pump And Dump" Scam

It's common to see messages posted online that urge readers to buy a stock quickly or tell you to sell before the price goes down. Often the writers will claim to have "inside" information about an impending development or to use an "infallible" combination of economic and stock market data to pick stocks. In reality, they may be insiders or paid promoters who stand to gain by selling their shares after the stock price is pumped up by gullible investors. Once these fraudsters sell their shares and stop hyping the stock, the price typically falls and investors lose their money. Fraudsters frequently use this ploy with small, thinly-traded companies because it's easier to manipulate a stock when there's little or no information available about the company.

The Pyramid

Be wary of messages that read: "How To Make Big Money From Your Home Computer!!!" One online promoter claimed that investors could "turn $5 into $60,000 in just three to six weeks." In reality, this program was nothing more than an electronic version of the classic "pyramid" scheme in which participants attempt to make money solely by recruiting new participants into the program.

The "Risk-Free" Fraud

"Exciting, Low-Risk Investment Opportunities" to participate in exotic-sounding investments such as wireless cable projects, prime bank securities, and eel farms have been offered through the Internet. But no investment is risk-free. And sometimes the investment products touted do not even exist; they're merely scams. Be wary of opportunities that promise spectacular profits or "guaranteed" returns. If the deal sounds too good to be true, then it probably is.

$ Off-shore Frauds

At one time, offshore schemes targeting U.S. investors cost a great deal of money and were difficult to carry out. Conflicting time zones, differing currencies, and the high costs of international telephone calls and overnight mailings made it difficult for fraudsters to prey on U.S. residents. But the Internet has removed those obstacles. Be extra careful when considering any investment opportunity that comes from another country, because it's difficult for U.S. law enforcement agencies to investigate and prosecute foreign frauds.

The SEC Is Tracking Fraud

The SEC actively investigates allegations of Internet investment fraud and, in many cases, has taken quick action to stop scams. We've also coordinated with federal and state criminal authorities to put Internet fraudsters in jail. Here's a sampling of recent cases in which the SEC took action to fight Internet fraud:

Francis A. Tribble and Sloane Fitzgerald, Inc. sent more than six million unsolicited e-mails, built bogus web sites, and distributed an online newsletter over a ten-month period to promote two small, thinly traded "microcap" companies. Because they failed to tell investors that the companies they were touting had agreed to pay them in cash and securities, the SEC sued both Tribble and Sloane to stop them from violating the law again and imposed a $15,000 penalty on Tribble. Their massive spamming campaign triggered the largest number of complaints to the SEC's online Enforcement Complaint Center.

Charles O. Huttoe and twelve other defendants secretly distributed to friends and family nearly 42 million shares of Systems of Excellence Inc., known by its ticker symbol "SEXI." Huttoe drove up the price of SEXI shares through false press releases claiming non-existent multi-million dollar sales, an acquisition that had not occurred, and revenue projections that had no basis in reality. He also bribed co-defendant SGA Goldstar to tout SEXI to subscribers of SGA Goldstar's online "Whisper Stocks" newsletter. The SEC obtained court orders freezing Huttoe's assets and those of various others who participated in the scheme or who received fraud proceeds. Six people, including Huttoe and Theodore R. Melcher, Jr., the author of the online newsletter, were also convicted of criminal violations. Both Huttoe and Melcher were sentenced to federal prison. The SEC has thus far recovered approximately $11 million in illegal profits from the various defendants.

Matthew Bowin recruited investors for his company, *Interactive Products and Services*, in a direct public offering done entirely over the Internet. He raised $190,000 from 150 investors. But instead of using the money to build the company, Bowin pocketed the proceeds and bought groceries and stereo equipment. The SEC sued Bowin in a civil case, and the Santa Cruz, CA District Attorney's Office prosecuted him criminally. He was convicted of 54 felony counts and sentenced to 10 years in jail.

IVT Systems solicited investments to finance the construction of an ethanol plant in the Dominican Republic. The Internet solicitations promised a return of 50% or more with no reasonable basis for the prediction. Their literature contained lies about contracts with well known companies and omitted other important information for investors. After the SEC filed a complaint, they agreed to stop breaking the law.

Gene Block and Renate Haag were caught offering "prime bank" securities, a type of security that doesn't even exist. They collected over $3.5 million by promising to double investors' money in four months. The SEC has frozen their assets and stopped them from continuing their fraud.

Daniel Odulo was stopped from soliciting investors for a proposed eel farm. Odulo promised investors a "whopping 20% return," claiming that the investment was "low risk." When he was caught by the SEC, he consented to the court order stopping him from breaking the securities laws.

If you believe that you have been the victim of a securities-related fraud, through the Internet or otherwise, or if you believe that any person or entity may have violated or is currently violating the federal securities laws, you can submit a complaint by sending an e-mail to *enforcement@sec.gov*.

INVESTigate
Before You INVEST!

- Download and print a hard copy of any on-line solicitation that you are considering. Make sure you catch the Internet address (URL) and note the date and time that you saw the offer. Save this in case you need it later.
- Don't assume that people on-line are who they claim they are. The investment that sounds so good may be a figment of their imagination, or they may be paid to promote it.
- Ask the on-line promoter whether – and how much – they've been paid to tout the opportunity.
- Ask the on-line promoter where the company is incorporated. Call that state's secretary of state and ask if the company is incorporated with them and has a current annual report on file. Also, check the SEC's EDGAR database.
- Don't believe everything you read on-line. Take the time to investigate a possible investment opportunity before you hand over your hard-earned money.
- Check with your state securities regulator or the SEC and ask if they have received any complaints about the company, its managers, or the promoter.

- Ask for other sources of information at your local public library. For example, there are resources that provide information about the company, such as a payment analysis, credit report, lawsuits, liens, or judgments.
- Before you invest, always obtain written financial information, such as a prospectus, annual report, offering circular, and financial statements. Compare the written information to what you've read on-line and watch out if you're told that no information is available.
- Don't assume that your access provider or on-line service has approved or even screened the investment. Anyone can set up a web site or advertise on-line, often without any check of its legitimacy or truthfulness.
- Check with a trusted financial advisor, your broker, or attorney about any investment you learn about on-line.

Have You Run Into A Problem?

Don't be embarrassed if you think you've been duped – you are not alone. Complain promptly. By complaining early you will have a better chance of getting your money back, protecting your legal rights, preventing others from losing money, and assisting securities regulators in stopping investment fraud.

http://www.sec.gov/investor/pubs/cyberfraud/investigate.htm

Tips for Checking Out Newsletters

Find out whether the newsletter received payment to "tout" or recommend the stock and, if so, what it received and from whom.

Because the U.S. Constitution's First Amendment protects freedom of speech, the SEC cannot simply prohibit newsletters from recommending or touting particular stocks. But when newsletters receive payment for touting, the securities laws require them to disclose specifically who paid them, the amount, and the type of payment (cash, stock, or some other thing of value).

Read carefully what the newsletter says about payments it receives.

Be suspicious of newsletters that do not specifically disclose these items: who paid them, the amount, and the type of payment. The following examples raise red flags because they do not contain specific information:

- "From time to time, XYZ Newsletter may receive compensation from companies we write about."
- "From time to time, XYZ Newsletter or its officers, directors, or staff may hold stock in some of the companies we write about."
- "XYZ Newsletter receives fees from the companies we write about in our newsletter."

Think twice about newsletters that bury their disclosures or put them in tiny, hard-to-read typeface. Legitimate online newsletters that have been paid to tout stocks will clearly and specifically tell investors who paid them, the amount, and the type of payment. Look for their disclosure statements in articles about particular companies or in a list or chart on their websites.

Independently investigate the company or investment opportunity.

Be wary of anyone who encourages you to invest in small, thinly-traded stocks that aren't well known and don't file reports with the SEC. Assume that everything you read about those companies in an online bulletin board, newsletter, or chat room is untrue until you prove by your own independent research that it isn't. Read the *tips* for assessing any investment opportunity.

Don't invest in small, thinly-traded companies unless you're prepared to lose every penny

Because small, thinly-traded companies are usually the most risky investments that you can make, you should always get as much written information as you can from the company and other independent sources. The SEC and your state's securities regulator should always be your first stops, but you may also want to visit your local library and talk with the librarian about other sources of information. There are also a number of commercial services that provide a constant stream of information about the financial condition of companies.

Check with the SEC or your state securities regulator to see if the newsletter has ever been in trouble

Whenever the SEC sues a newsletter or stock promoter, they issue a "litigation release" and post it on their web site. Check the Enforcement Division's home page to see whether they've brought action against a newsletter or stock promoter who's touting a stock. You can also search the SEC's non-EDGAR database for this information.

Your state securities regulator, which can be found at the website of the North American Securities Administrators Association, can tell you whether the broker pushing the stock or the broker's firm has a disciplinary history by checking the Central Registration Depository (CRD). To check the disciplinary history of the broker or firm that's touting the stock, use NASD's BrokerCheck website, or call NASD's BrokerCheck Program hotline at (800) 289-9999.

http://www.sec.gov/investor/pubs/cyberfraud/newsletter.htm

Ten Questions To Ask About Any Investment Opportunity

With any investment, whether promoted in person, by mail, telephone, or on the Internet, a wise investor should always slow down, ask questions, and get written information. Take notes so you have a record of what you were told, in case you have a dispute later.

1. Is the investment registered with the SEC and the state securities agency in the state where I live or is it subject to an exemption?

2. Is the person recommending this investment registered with my state securities agency? Is there a record of any complaints about this person?
3. How does this investment match my investment objectives?
4. Where is the company incorporated? Will you send me the latest reports that have been filed on this company?
5. What are the costs to buy, hold, and sell this investment? How easily can I sell?
6. Who is managing the investment? What experience do they have?
7. What is the risk that I could lose the money I invest?
8. What return can I expect on my money? When?
9. How long has the company been in business? Are they making money, and if so, how? What is their product or service? What other companies are in this business?
10. How can I get more information about this investment, such as audited financial statements?

Asking these questions before the fact will save a lot of money and avoid the difficulties of recovering and fixing the results of a poor dicision.

www.sec.gov/investor/pubs/cyberfraud/questions.htm

Be Alert for Telltale Signs of Online Investment Fraud

- Be wary of promises of quick profits, offers to share "inside" information, and pressure to invest before you have an opportunity to investigate.
- Be careful of promoters who use "aliases." Pseudonyms are common on-line, and some

salespeople will to try to hide their true identity. Look for other promotions by the same person.

- Words like "guarantee," "high return," "limited offer," or "as safe as a C.D." may be a red flag. No financial investment is "risk free" and a high rate of return means greater risk.
- Watch out for offshore scams and investment opportunities in other countries. When you send your money abroad, and something goes wrong, it's more difficult to find out what happened and to locate your money.
- If a company is not registered or has not filed a "Form D" with the SEC, visit the website of the North American Securities Administrators Association to find your state securities regulator.

Remember, if it sounds too good to be true, it probably is!

www.sec.gov/investor/pubs/cyberfraud/signs.htm

You've Got Spam: How to "Can" Unwanted E-mail

Do you receive lots of junk e-mail messages from people you don't know? It's no surprise if you do. As more people use e-mail, marketers are increasingly using e-mail messages to pitch their products and services. Some consumers find unsolicited commercial e-mail, also known as "spam", annoying and time consuming; others have lost money to bogus offers that arrived in their e-mail in-box.

Typically, an e-mail spammer buys a list of e-mail addresses from a list broker, who compiles it by "harvesting" addresses from the Internet. If your e-mail address appears in a newsgroup posting, on a website, in a chat room, or in an online service's membership directory, it may find its way onto these lists. The marketer then uses special software that can send hundreds of thousands, even millions of e-mail messages to the addresses at the click of a mouse.

How Can I Reduce the Amount of Spam that I Receive?

Try not to display your e-mail address in public. That includes newsgroup postings, chat rooms, websites or in an online service's membership directory. You may want to opt out of member directories for your online services; spammers may use them to harvest addresses.

Check the privacy policy when you submit your address to a website. See if it allows the company to sell your address. You may want to opt out of this provision, if possible, or not submit your address at all to websites that won't protect it.

Read and understand the entire form before you transmit personal information through a website. Some websites allow you to opt out of receiving e-mail from their "partners" but you may have to uncheck a preselected box if you want to opt out.

Decide if you want to use two e-mail addresses; one for personal messages and one for newsgroups and chat rooms. You also might consider using a disposable e-mail address service that creates a separate e-mail address that forwards to your permanent account. If one of the disposable addresses begins to receive spam, you can shut it off without affecting your permanent address.

Use a unique e-mail address. Your choice of e-mail addresses may affect the amount of spam you receive. Spammers use "dictionary attacks" to sort through possible name combinations at large ISPs or e-mail services, hoping to find a valid address. Thus, a common name such as jdoe may get more spam than a more unique name like jd51x02oe. Of course, there is a downside - it's harder to remember an unusual e-mail address.

Use an e-mail filter. Check your e-mail account to see if it provides a tool to filter out potential spam or a way to channel spam into a bulk e-mail folder. You might want to consider these options when you're choosing which Internet Service Provider (ISP) to use.

What Can I Do With the Spam in my In-Box?

Report it to the Federal Trade Commission. Send a copy of unwanted or deceptive messages to *spam@uce.gov*. The FTC uses the unsolicited e-mails stored in this database to pursue law enforcement actions against people who send deceptive spam e-mail.

Let the FTC know if a "remove me" request is not honored. If you want to complain about a removal link that doesn't work or not being able to unsubscribe from a list, you can fill out the FTC's online complaint form at *www.ftc.gov*. Your complaint will be added to the FTC's Consumer Sentinel database and made available to hundreds of law enforcement and consumer protection agencies.

Whenever you complain about spam, it's important to include the full e-mail header. The information in the header makes it possible for consumer protection agencies to follow up on your complaint.

Send a copy of the spam to your ISP's abuse desk. Often the e-mail address is abuse@yourispname.com or _postmaster@yourispname.com_. By doing this, you can let the ISP know about the spam problem on their system and help them to stop it in the future. Make sure to include a copy of the spam, along with the full e-mail header. At the top of the message, state that you're complaining about being spammed.

Complain to the sender's ISP. Most ISPs want to cut off spammers who abuse their system. Again, make sure to include a copy of the message and header information and state that you're complaining about spam.

How Can I Avoid Spam Scams?

The FTC suggests that you treat commercial e-mail solicitations the same way you would treat an unsolicited telemarketing sales call. Don't believe promises from strangers. Greet money making opportunities that arrive at your in box with skepticism. Most of the time, these are old-fashioned scams delivered via the newest technology.

Here are some of the most common scam offers likely to arrive by e-mail:

Chain letters

Chain letters that involve money or valuable items and promise big returns are illegal. If you start one or send one on, you are breaking the law. Chances are you will receive little or no money back on your "investment." Despite the claims, a chain letter will never make you rich. For more information on chain e-mails, check out *www.ftc.gov/bcp/conline/pubs/alerts/chainalrt.shtm*.

Work-At-Home Schemes

Not all work at home opportunities deliver on their promises. Many ads omit the fact that you may have to work many hours without pay. Or they don't disclose all the costs you will have to pay. Countless work at home schemes require you to spend your own money to place newspaper ads; make photocopies; or buy the envelopes, paper, stamps, and other supplies or equipment you need to do the job. The companies sponsoring the ads also may demand that you pay for instructions or "tutorial" software. Consumers deceived by these ads have lost thousands of dollars, in addition to their time and energy.

Weight Loss Claims

Programs or products that promote easy or effortless long-term weight loss don't work. Taking off weight, and keeping it off, requires exercise and permanent changes in your diet. All the testimonials and guarantees in your e-mail are not worth the space they take up on your hard drive.

Credit Repair Offers

Ignore offers to erase accurate negative information from your credit record. There's no legal way to do that.

Advance Fee Loan Scams

Be wary of promises to provide a loan for a fee, regardless of your past credit history. Remember, legitimate banks don't issue credit cards without first checking your credit.

Adult Entertainment

You may get an e-mail from an adult entertainment site that claims to offer content for "free" and doesn't require a credit card number for access. All you have to do is download a "viewer" or "dialer" program. However, once the program is downloaded onto your computer, it may disconnect your Internet connection and reconnect to an international long distance phone number, at rates between $2 and $7 a minute. Be skeptical when you see opportunities to view "free" content on the web.

The FTC works for the consumer to prevent fraudulent, deceptive, and unfair business practices in the marketplace and to provide information to help consumers spot, stop, and avoid them. To file a complaint or to get free information on consumer issues, visit *www.ftc.gov* or call toll-free, 1-877-FTC-HELP (1-877-382-4357); TTY: 1-866-653-4261. The FTC enters Internet, telemarketing, identity theft, and other fraud-related complaints into Consumer Sentinel, a secure online database available to hundreds of civil and criminal law enforcement agencies in the U.S. and abroad.

Resources

There are many great sources of safety and security information on the Internet, Please check the Web Sites of the National Cyber Security Alliance's members and other organizations for more information:

General Information:

Microsoft *(www.microsoft.com/protect)*

Center for Democracy in Technology *(www.cdt.org)*

Electronic Privacy Information Center *(www.epic.org)*

Privacy Rights Clearinghouse *(www.privacyrights.org)*

NCSA *(www.staysafeonline.info)*

National Consumers League *(www.nclnet.org)*

GetNetWise *(www.getnetwise.org)*

Federal Trade Commission *(www.ftc.gov/infosecurity)*

United States Computer Emergency Rediness Team *(www.us-cert.gov)*

U. S. Federal Government Resources *(www.usa.gov)*

www.OnGuardOnline.gov
http://www.ftc.gov/bcp/edu/microsites/idtheft// OnGuard Online provides practical tips from the federal government and the technology industry to help you be on guard against Internet fraud, secure your computer, and protect your personal information.

To keep up to date with information about the latest computer threats, sign up for alerts from the Department of Homeland Security at *http://www.us-cert.gov/*.

For updates:

Microsoft *(www.windowsupdate.microsoft.com)*

Security tips:

NSCA *(www.staysafeonline.info/practices/index.html)*

Firewall software resources:

Internet Security Systems *(www.iss.net)*
McAfee *(www.mcafee.com)*
Symantec *(www.symantec.com)*
Techguard Security *(www.techguardsecurity.com)*
Tumbleweed *(www.tumbleweed.com)*

Anti-virus software resources:

McAfee *(www.mcafee.com)*
Symantec *(www.symantec.com)*
Tumbleweed *(www.tumbleweed.com)*

Reference material and portions of this book originated with or were sourced, contributed and/or reviewed by the following;

Federal Trade Commission
National Consumers League
U.S. Securities and Exchange Commission
Federal Citizen Information Center
National Cyber Security Alliance
Microsoft Corporation

.

www.ingramcontent.com/pod-product-compliance
Lightning Source LLC
Chambersburg PA
CBHW071552080326
40690CB00056B/1803